# The Key Facts™ on Ecuador

*Essential Information on Ecuador*

By Patrick W. Nee

The Internationalist®
www.internationalist.com

**The Internationalist®**

*International Business, Investment, and Travel*

**Published by:**

The Internationalist Publishing Company

96 Walter Street/ Suite 200

Boston, MA 02131, USA

Tel: 617-354-7722

www.internationalist.com

PN@internationalist.com

The Internationalist is a Registered Trademark. "Key Facts" and "The Internationalist Business Guides" are Trademarks of The Internationalist Publishing Company.

All Rights are reserved under International, Pan-American, and Pan-Asian Conventions. No part of this book may be reproduced in any form without the written permission of the publisher. All rights vigorously enforced

# *Table Of Contents*

Chapter 1: Background

Chapter 2: Geography

Chapter 3: People and Society

Chapter 4: Government and Key Leaders

Chapter 5: Economy

Chapter 6: Energy

Chapter 7: Communications

Chapter 8: Transportation

Chapter 9: Military

Chapter 10: Transnational Issues

Map of Ecuador

# Chapter 1: Background

What is now Ecuador formed part of the northern Inca Empire until the Spanish conquest in 1533. Quito became a seat of Spanish colonial government in 1563 and part of the Viceroyalty of New Granada in 1717. The territories of the Viceroyalty - New Granada (Colombia), Venezuela, and Quito - gained their independence between 1819 and 1822 and formed a federation known as Gran Colombia. When Quito withdrew in 1830, the traditional name was changed in favor of the "Republic of the Equator." Between 1904 and 1942, Ecuador lost territories in a series of conflicts with its neighbors. A border war with Peru that flared in 1995 was resolved in 1999. Although Ecuador marked 30 years of civilian governance in 2004, the period was marred by political instability. Protests in Quito contributed to the mid-term ouster of three of Ecuador's last four democratically elected presidents. In late 2008, voters approved a new constitution, Ecuador's 20th since gaining independence. General elections were held in February 2013, and voters re-elected President Rafael CORREA.

# Chapter 2: Geography

**Location:**

Western South America, bordering the Pacific Ocean at the Equator, between Colombia and Peru

**Geographic coordinates:**

2 00 S, 77 30 W

**Map references:**

South America

**Area:**

total: 283,561 sq km

country comparison to the world: 74

land: 276,841 sq km

water: 6,720 sq km

note: includes Galapagos Islands

**Area - comparative:**

Slightly smaller than Nevada

**Land boundaries:**

total: 2,010 km

border countries: Colombia 590 km, Peru 1,420 km

**Coastline:**

2,237 km

**Maritime claims:**
>territorial sea: 200 nm
>
>continental shelf: 100 nm from 2,500-m isobath

**Climate:**
>Tropical along coast, becoming cooler inland at higher elevations; tropical in Amazonian jungle lowlands

**Terrain:**
>coastal plain (costa), inter-Andean central highlands (sierra), and flat to rolling eastern jungle (oriente)

**Elevation extremes:**
>lowest point: Pacific Ocean 0 m
>
>highest point: Cimborazo 6,267 m
>
>note: due to the fact that the earth is not a perfect sphere and has an equatorial bulge, the highest point on the planet furthest from its center is Mount Chimborazo not Mount Everest, which is merely the highest peak above sea-level

**Natural resources:**
>Petroleum, fish, timber, hydropower

**Land use:**
>arable land: 4.51%

permanent crops: 5.38%

other: 90.11% (2011)

**Irrigated land:**

8,534 sq km (2003)

**Total renewable water resources:**

424.4 cu km (2011)

**Freshwater withdrawal (domestic/industrial/agricultural):**

total: 9.92 cu km/yr (13%/6%/81%)

per capita: 716.1 cu m/yr (2005)

**Natural hazards:**

frequent earthquakes; landslides; volcanic activity; floods; periodic droughts
**volcanism:** volcanic activity concentrated along the Andes Mountains; Sangay (elev. 5,230 m), which erupted in 2010, is mainland Ecuador's most active volcano; other historically active volcanoes in the Andes include Antisana, Cayambe, Chacana, Cotopaxi, Guagua Pichincha, Reventador, Sumaco, and Tungurahua; Fernandina (elev. 1,476 m), a shield volcano that last erupted in 2009, is the most active of the many Galapagos volcanoes; other historically active Galapagos volcanoes include Wolf, Sierra Negra, Cerro Azul, Pinta, Marchena, and Santiago

**Environment - current issues:**
deforestation; soil erosion; desertification; water pollution; pollution from oil production wastes in ecologically sensitive areas of the Amazon Basin and Galapagos Islands

**Environment - international agreements:**
party to: Antarctic-Environmental Protocol, Antarctic Treaty, Biodiversity, Climate Change, Climate Change-Kyoto Protocol, Desertification, Endangered Species, Hazardous Wastes, Ozone Layer Protection, Ship Pollution, Tropical Timber 83, Tropical Timber 94, Wetlands
signed, but not ratified: none of the selected agreements

**Geography - note:**
Cotopaxi in Andes is highest active volcano in world

# Chapter 3: People and Society

**Nationality:**
>noun: Ecuadorian(s)
>adjective: Ecuadorian

**Ethnic groups:**
>mestizo (mixed Amerindian and white) 71.9%, Montubio 7.4%, Afroecuadorian 7.2%, Amerindian 7%, white 6.1%, other 0.4% (2010 census)

**Languages:**
>Spanish (official), indigenous (Quechua, Shuar)

**Religions:**
>Roman Catholic 95%, other 5%

**Population:**
>15,439,429 (July 2013 est.)
>country comparison to the world: 68

**Age structure:**
>0-14 years: 29% (male 2,284,815/female 2,193,648)
>15-24 years: 18.7% (male 1,462,025/female 1,427,181)
>25-54 years: 38.7% (male 2,908,224/female 3,061,896)

55-64 years: 6.9% (male 524,574/female 540,074)

65 years and over: 6.7% (male 496,557/female 540,435) (2013 est.)

**Median age:**

total: 26.3 years

male: 25.7 years

female: 26.9 years (2013 est.)

**Population growth rate:**

1.4% (2013 est.)

country comparison to the world: 87

**Birth rate:**

19.23/1,000 population (2013 est.)

country comparison to the world: 92

**Death rate:**

5.03/1,000 population (2013 est.)

country comparison to the world: 185

**Net migration rate:**

-0.25 migrant(s)/1,000 population (2013 est.)

country comparison to the world: 122

**Urbanization:**

urban population: 67% of total population (2010)

rate of urbanization: 2% annual rate of change (2010-15 est.)

**Major urban areas - population:**
Guayaquil 2.634 million; QUITO (capital) 1.622 million (2011)

**Sex ratio:**
at birth: 1.05 male(s)/female
0-14 years: 1.04 male(s)/female
15-24 years: 1.02 male(s)/female
25-54 years: 0.95 male(s)/female
55-64 years: 0.98 male(s)/female
65 years and over: 0.92 male(s)/female
total population: 0.99 male(s)/female (2013 est.)

**Maternal mortality rate:**
110 deaths/100,000 live births (2010)
country comparison to the world: 67

**Infant mortality rate:**
total: 18.48 deaths/1,000 live births
country comparison to the world: 98
male: 21.73 deaths/1,000 live births
female: 15.07 deaths/1,000 live births (2013 est.)

**Life expectancy at birth:**
> total population: 76.15 years
> country comparison to the world: 84
> male: 73.2 years
> female: 79.25 years (2013 est.)

**Total fertility rate:**
> 2.33 children born/woman (2013 est.)
> country comparison to the world: 95

**Health expenditures:**
> 7.3% of GDP (2011)
> country comparison to the world: 79

**Physicians density:**
> 1.69 physicians/1,000 population (2009)

**Hospital bed density:**
> 1.6 beds/1,000 population (2010)

**Drinking water source:**
> improved:
>> *urban*: 96.5% of population
>> *rural*: 82.2% of population
>> *total*: 91.8% of population

unimproved:
    urban: 3.5% of population
    rural: 17.8% of population
    total: 8.2% of population (2011 est.)

**Sanitation facility access:**
  improved:
    urban: 96.2% of population
    rural: 86.1% of population
    total: 92.9% of population
  unimproved:
    urban: 3.8% of population
    rural: 13.9% of population
    total: 7.1% of population (2011 est.)

**HIV/AIDS - adult prevalence rate:**
  0.4% (2009 est.)
  country comparison to the world: 74

**HIV/AIDS - people living with HIV/AIDS:**
  37,000 (2009 est.)
  country comparison to the world: 63

**HIV/AIDS - deaths:**
  2,200 (2009 est.)
  country comparison to the world: 54

**Major infectious diseases:**
    degree of risk: high
    food or waterborne diseases: bacterial diarrhea, hepatitis A, and typhoid fever
    vectorborne diseases: dengue feverand malaria

**Obesity - adult prevalence rate:**
    21.4% (2008)
    country comparison to the world: 86

**Education expenditures:**
    4.9% of GDP (2010)
    country comparison to the world: 79

**Literacy:**
    definition: age 15 and over can read and write
    total population: 91.6%
    male: 93.1%
    female: 90.2% (2011 est.)

**School life expectancy (primary to tertiary education):**
    total: 14 years
    male: 13 years
    female: 14 years (2008)

**Unemployment, youth ages 15-24:**
    total: 14.1%
    country comparison to the world: 91
    male: 11.7%
    female: 18.1% (2009)

# Chapter 4: Government and Key Leaders

**Country name:**
> conventional long form: Republic of Ecuador
> conventional short form: Ecuador
> local long form: Republica del Ecuador
> local short form: Ecuador

**Government type:**
> Republic

**Capital:**
> name: Quito
> geographic coordinates: 0 13 S, 78 30 W
> time difference: UTC-5 (same time as Washington, DC during Standard Time)

**Administrative divisions:**
> 24 provinces (provincias, singular - provincia); Azuay, Bolivar, Canar, Carchi, Chimborazo, Cotopaxi, El Oro, Esmeraldas, Galapagos, Guayas, Imbabura, Loja, Los Rios, Manabi, Morona-Santiago, Napo, Orellana, Pastaza, Pichincha, Santa Elena, Santo Domingo de los Tsachilas, Sucumbios, Tungurahua, Zamora-Chinchipe

**Independence:**
24 May 1822 (from Spain)

**National holiday:**
Independence Day (independence of Quito), 10 August (1809)

**Constitution:**
Many previous; latest approved 20 October 2008; amended 2011 (2011)

**Legal system:**
Civil law based on the Chilean civil code with modifications

**International law organization participation:**
Has not submitted an ICJ jurisdiction declaration; accepts ICCt jurisdiction

**Suffrage:**
18-65 years of age, universal and compulsory; 16-18, over 65, and other eligible voters, optional

**Executive branch:**

chief of state: President Rafael CORREA Delgado (since 15 January 2007); Vice President Lenin MORENO Garces (since 15 January 2007); note - the president is both the chief of state and head of government

head of government: President Rafael CORREA Delgado (since 15 January 2007); Vice President Lenin MORENO Garces (since 15 January 2007)

cabinet: Cabinet appointed by the president

elections: the president and vice president elected on the same ticket by popular vote for a four-year term and can be re-elected for another consecutive term; election last held on 17 February 2013 (next to be held in 2017)

election results: President Rafael CORREA Delgado reelected president; percent of vote - Rafael CORREA Delgado 57.2%, Guillermo LASSO 22.7%, Lucio GUTIERREZ 6.8%, Mauricio RODAS 3.9%, other 9.4%

**Legislative branch:**
unicameral National Assembly or Asamblea Nacional (137 seats; members are elected through a party-list proportional representation system to serve four-year terms)
elections: last held on 17 February 2013 (next to be held in 2017)
election results: percent of vote by party - NA; seats by party - PAIS 100, CREO 11, PSC 6, AVANZA 5, MUPP 5, PSP 5, other 5; note - defections by members of National Assembly are commonplace, resulting in frequent changes in the numbers of seats held by the various parties

**Judicial branch:**
Highest court(s): National Court of Justice or Corte Nacional de Justicia (consists of 21 judges including a chief justice and organized into 5 specialized chambers); Constitutional Court or Corte Constitutional (consists of 11 judges)

Judge selection and term of offfice: justices of National Court of Justice elected by the Judiciary Council, a 9-member independent body of professionals; judges elected for 9-year, non-renewable terms, with one-third of the judges renewed every 3 years; Constitutional Court judges appointed by the National Assembly from candidates selected by the president, Supreme Court, and other government officials; judges appointed for 2-year terms

subordinate courts: Fiscal Tribunal; Superior Court (one for each province); lower provincial and cantonal courts

**Political parties and leaders:**
Alianza PAIS movement [Rafael Vicente CORREA Delgado]
Avanza Party or AVANZA [Ramiro GONZALEZ]
Breakaway Party [Martha ROLDOS]
Creating Opportunities Movement or CREO [Guillermo LASSO]
Institutional Renewal and National Action Party or PRIAN [Alvaro NOBOA]
Pachakutik Plurinational Unity Movement or MUPP [Rafael ANTUNI]
Patriotic Society Party or PSP [Lucio GUTIERREZ Borbua]

Plurinational Union Movement of the Left [Alberto ACOSTA]
Roldosist Party or PRE [Abdala BUCARAM Pulley, director]
Social Christian Party or PSC [Pascual DEL CIOPPO]
Socialist Party
Society United for More Action or SUMA [Mauricio RODAS]
Warrior's Spirit Movement [Jaime NEBOT]

**Political pressure groups and leaders:**

Confederation of Indigenous Nationalities of Ecuador or CONAIE [Humberto CHOLANGO]
Federation of Indigenous Evangelists of Ecuador or FEINE [Manuel CHUGCHILAN, president]
National Federation of Indigenous Afro-Ecuatorianos and Peasants or FENOCIN
National Teacher's Union or UNE [Mariana PALLASCO]

**International organization participation:**

CAN, CD, CELAC, FAO, G-11, G-77, IADB, IAEA, IBRD, ICAO, ICC (national committees), ICRM, IDA, IFAD, IFC, IFRCS, IHO, ILO, IMF, IMO, Interpol, IOC, IOM, IPU, ISO, ITSO, ITU, ITUC (NGOs), LAES, LAIA, Mercosur (associate), MIGA, MINUSTAH, NAM, OAS, OPANAL, OPCW, OPEC, PCA, UN, UNAMID, UNASUR,

UNCTAD, UNESCO, UNHCR, UNIDO, Union Latina, UNMIL, UNMISS, UNOCI, UNWTO, UPU, WCO, WFTU (NGOs), WHO, WIPO, WMO, WTO

**Diplomatic representation in the US:**

chief of mission: Ambassador Saskia Nathalie CELY Suarez (since 2 December 2011)

chancery: 1050 30th Street, NW, Washington, DC 20007

telephone: [1] (202) 465-8140

FAX: [1] (202) 333-2893

Consulate(s) general: Atlanta, Boston, Chicago, Houston, Los Angeles, Miami, New Haven (CT), New Orleans, New York, Newark (NJ), Phoenix, San Francisco, San Juan (Puerto Rico)

**Diplomatic representation from the US:**

chief of mission: Ambassador Adam E. NAMM (since 26 April 2012)

embassy: Avenida Avigiras E12-170 y Avenida Eloy Alfaro, Quito

mailing address: Avenida Guayacanes N52-205 y Avenida Avigiras

telephone: [593] (2) 398-5000

FAX: [593] (2) 398-5100

**Key Leaders:**

**Pres.**
Rafael CORREA Delgado

**Vice Pres.**
Jorge GLAS Espinel

**Min. of Agriculture, Livestock, Fisheries, & Aquaculture**
Javier PONCE Cevallos

**Min. of Culture**
Francisco VELASCO Andrade

**Min. of Economic & Social Inclusion**
Doris SOLIZ Carrion

**Min. of Education**
Augusto ESPINOSA

**Min. of Electricity & Renewable Energy**
Esteban ALBORNOZ

**Min. of Environment**
Lorena TAPIA Nunez

**Min. of Finance**
Fausto HERRERA

**Min. of Foreign Relations, Foreign Trade, & Integration**
Ricardo PATINO Aroca

**Min. of Industry & Competitiveness**
Ramiro GONZALEZ Jaramillo

**Min. of Interior**
Jose SERRANO

**Min. of Justice & Human Rights**
Lenin LARA

**Min. of Labor Relations**
Jose FRANCISCO Vacas

**Min. of Nonrenewable Natural Resources**
Pedro MERIZALDE Pavon

**Min. of National Defense**
Maria Fernanda ESPINOSA Garces

**Min. of Public Health**
Carina VANCE

**Min. of Sports**
Jose FRANCISCO Cevallos

**Min. of Telecommunication & Information**
Jaime GUERRERO Ruiz

**Min. of Tourism**
Vinicio ALVARADO Espinel

**Min. of Transportation & Public Works**
Maria de los ANGELES Duarte

**Min. of Urban Development & Housing**
Diego AULESTIA

**Min. Coordinator of Economic Policy**
Patricio RIVERA

**Min. Coordinator of Internal & External Security Policy**
Homero ARELLANO, Adm. (Ret.)

**Min. Coordinator of Natural & Cultural Heritage**
Velasco ANDRADE

**Min. Coordinator of Policy**
Betty TOLA

**Min. Coordinator of Production**
Richard ESPINOSA

**Min. Coordinator of Social Development**
Cecilia VACA Jones

**Min. Coordinator of Strategic Sectors**
Rafael PROVEDA Bonilla

**National Sec. of Planning & Development**
Pabel MUNOZ

**Sec. Gen. of Public Admin.**
Cristian CASTILLO Penaherrera

**Pres., Central Bank**
Diego MARTINEZ

**Ambassador to the US**

Nathalie CELY Suarez

**Permanent Representative to the UN, New York**

Julio Xavier LASSO Mendoza

**Flag description:**

three horizontal bands of yellow (top, double width), blue, and red with the coat of arms superimposed at the center of the flag; the flag retains the three main colors of the banner of Gran Columbia, the South American republic that broke up in 1830; the yellow color represents sunshine, grain, and mineral wealth, blue the sky, sea, and rivers, and red the blood of patriots spilled in the struggle for freedom and justice

**National symbol(s):**

Andean condor

**National anthem:**

name: "Salve, Oh Patria!" (We Salute You Our Homeland)

# Chapter 5: Economy

**Economy - overview:**
Ecuador is substantially dependent on its petroleum resources, which have accounted for more than half of the country's export earnings and approximately two-fifths of public sector revenues in recent years. In 1999/2000, Ecuador's economy suffered from a banking crisis, with GDP contracting by 5.3% and poverty increasing significantly. In March 2000, the Congress approved a series of structural reforms that also provided for the adoption of the US dollar as legal tender. Dollarization stabilized the economy, and positive growth returned in the years that followed, helped by high oil prices, remittances, and increased non-traditional exports. From 2002-06 the economy grew an average of 4.3% per year, the highest five-year average in 25 years. After moderate growth in 2007, the economy reached a growth rate of 6.4% in 2008, buoyed by high global petroleum prices and increased public sector investment. President Rafael CORREA, who took office in January 2007, defaulted in December 2008 on Ecuador's sovereign debt, which, with a total face

value of approximately US$3.2 billion, represented about 30% of Ecuador's public external debt. In May 2009, Ecuador bought back 91% of its "defaulted" bonds via an international reverse auction. Economic policies under the CORREA administration - for example, an announcement in late 2009 of its intention to terminate 13 bilateral investment treaties, including one with the United States - have generated economic uncertainty and discouraged private investment. The Ecuadorian economy slowed to 1% growth in 2009 due to the global financial crisis and to the sharp decline in world oil prices and remittance flows. Growth picked up to a 3.3% rate in 2010 and nearly 8% in 2011, before falling to 5% in 2012. China has become Ecuador's largest foreign lender since Quito defaulted in 2008, allowing the government to maintain a high rate of social spending; Ecuador contracted with the Chinese government for more than $9 billion in oil for cash and project loans as of December 2012.

**GDP (purchasing power parity):**
>$149.5 billion (2012 est.)
>
>country comparison to the world: 62
>
>$142.2 billion (2011 est.)
>
>$131.9 billion (2010 est.)
>
>note: data are in 2012 US dollars

**GDP (official exchange rate):**
>$82.9 billion (2012 est.)

**GDP - real growth rate:**
>5.1% (2012 est.)
>
>country comparison to the world: 67
>
>7.8% (2011 est.)
>
>3% (2010 est.)

**GDP - per capita (PPP):**
>$10,200 (2012 est.)
>
>country comparison to the world: 117
>
>$9,900 (2011 est.)
>
>$9,300 (2010 est.)
>
>note: data are in 2012 US dollars

**GDP - composition by sector:**
>agriculture: 5.9%
>
>industry: 35.2%
>
>services: 58.8% (2012 est.)

**Labor force:**
4.769 million (2012 est.)
country comparison to the world: 81

**Labor force - by occupation:**
agriculture: 27.6%
industry: 18.8%
services: 53.6% (2010 est.)

**Unemployment rate:**
4.9% (2012 est.)
country comparison to the world: 43
6% (2011 est.)

**Population below poverty line:**
27.3% (December 2012 est.)

**Household income or consumption by percentage share:**
lowest 10%: 1.4%
highest 10%: 38.3%
note: data for urban households only (2010 est.)

**Distribution of family income - Gini index:**
47.7 (December 2012)
country comparison to the world: 27
50.5 (2006)
Note: data are for urban households

**Budget:**
revenues: $34.53 billion
expenditures: $35.48 billion (2012 est.)

**Taxes and other revenues:**
41.7% of GDP (2012 est.)
country comparison to the world: 36

**Budget surplus (+) or deficit (-):**
-1.1% of GDP (2012 est.)
country comparison to the world: 65

**Public debt:**
21% of GDP (2012 est.)
country comparison to the world: 129
17.8% of GDP (2011 est.)

**Inflation rate (consumer prices):**
3.2% (2012 est.)
country comparison to the world: 101
3.4% (2011 est.)

**Fiscal year:**
Calendar year

**Central bank discount rate:**
8.17% (31 December 2011)
country comparison to the world: 30
8.68% (31 December 2010 est.)

**Commercial bank prime lending rate:**
8.17% (31 December 2012 est.)
country comparison to the world: 112
8.35% (31 December 2011 est.)

**Stock of narrow money:**
$7.801 billion (31 December 2012 est.)
country comparison to the world: 86
$6.943 billion (31 December 2011 est.)

**Stock of broad money:**
$26.55 billion (31 December 2011 est.)
country comparison to the world: 78
$22.18 billion (31 December 2001 est.)

**Stock of domestic credit:**
$22.5 billion (31 December 2012 est.)
country comparison to the world: 74
$20.05 billion (31 December 2011 est.)

**Market value of publicly traded shares:**
$5.779 billion (31 December 2011)
country comparison to the world: 83
$5.263 billion (31 December 2010)
$4.248 billion (31 December 2009)

**Current account balance:**
> -177 million (2012 est.)
> country comparison to the world: 78
> $-225 million (2011 est.)

**Exports:**
> $24.65 billion (2012 est.)
> country comparison to the world: 72
> $23.08 billion (2011 est.)

**Exports - commodities:**
> Petroleum, bananas, cut flowers, shrimp, cacao, coffee, wood, fish

**Exports - partners:**
> US 37.3%, Chile 8.1%, Peru 6.5%, Japan 4.5%, Russia 4.5%, Colombia 4% (2012)

**Imports:**
> $24.58 billion (2012 est.)
> country comparison to the world: 70
> $23.24 billion (2011 est.)

**Imports - commodities:**
> Industrial materials, fuels and lubricants, nondurable consumer goods

**Imports - partners:**
> US 28.4%, China 11.3%, Colombia 8.8%, Peru 4.5% (2012)

**Reserves of foreign exchange and gold:**

$2.483 billion (31 December 2012 est.)

country comparison to the world: 117

$2.958 billion (31 December 2011 est.)

**Debt - external:**

$17.68 billion (31 December 2012 est.)

country comparison to the world: 81

$16.5 billion (31 December 2011 est.)

**Stock of direct foreign investment - at home:**

$17.3 billion (31 December 2012 est.)

country comparison to the world: 73

$16.71 billion (31 December 2011 est.)

**Stock of direct foreign investment - abroad:**

$6.33 billion (31 December 2012 est.)

country comparison to the world: 62

$6.33 billion (31 December 2011 est.)

**Exchange rates:**

The US dollar became Ecuador's currency in 2001

# Chapter 6: Energy

**Electricity - production:**
    21.84 billion kWh (2011 est.)
    country comparison to the world: 70

**Electricity - consumption:**
    14.92 billion kWh (2010 est.)
    country comparison to the world: 76

**Electricity - exports:**
    14.1 million kWh (2010 est.)
    country comparison to the world: 88

**Electricity - imports:**
    1.3 billion kWh (2010 est.)
    country comparison to the world: 60

**Electricity - installed generating capacity:**
    5.243 million kW (2010 est.)
    country comparison to the world: 75

**Electricity - from fossil fuels:**
    55.3% of total installed capacity (2010 est.)
    country comparison to the world: 142

**Electricity - from nuclear fuels:**
    0% of total installed capacity (2010 est.)
    country comparison to the world: 78

**Electricity - from hydroelectric plants:**
>42.8% of total installed capacity (2010 est.)
>country comparison to the world: 57

**Electricity - from other renewable sources:**
>2% of total installed capacity (2010 est.)
>country comparison to the world: 65

**Crude oil - production:**
>504,500 bbl/day (2012 est.)
>country comparison to the world: 31

**Crude oil - exports:**
>366,000 bbl/day (2012)
>country comparison to the world: 22

**Crude oil - imports:**
>154,000 bbl/day (2012 est.)
>country comparison to the world: 39

**Crude oil - proved reserves:**
>8.24 billion bbl (1 January 2013 es)
>country comparison to the world: 19

**Refined petroleum products - production:**
>198,700 bbl/day (2012 est.)
>country comparison to the world: 55

**Refined petroleum products - consumption:**
>280,000 bbl/day (2012 est.)
>country comparison to the world: 45

**Refined petroleum products - exports:**
>98,000 bbl/day (2012 est.)
>
>country comparison to the world: 70

**Refined petroleum products - imports:**
>111,000 bbl/day (2012 est.)
>
>country comparison to the world: 49

**Natural gas - production:**
>240 billion cu m (2011 est.)
>
>country comparison to the world: 76

**Natural gas - consumption:**
>330 million cu m (2010 est.)
>
>country comparison to the world: 99

**Natural gas - exports:**
>0 cu m (2011 est.)
>
>country comparison to the world: 92

**Natural gas - imports:**
>25,000 cu m (2012 est.)
>
>country comparison to the world: 77

**Natural gas - proved reserves:**
>6.994 billion cu m (1 January 2012 es)
>
>country comparison to the world: 86

**Carbon dioxide emissions from consumption of energy:**
>29.13 million Mt (2011 est.)
>
>country comparison to the world: 76

# Chapter 7: Communications

**Telephones - main lines in use:**
    2.31 million (2012)
    country comparison to the world: 54

**Telephones - mobile cellular:**
    16.457 million (2012)
    country comparison to the world: 56

**Telephone system:**
    general assessment: elementary fixed-line service, but increasingly sophisticated mobile-cellular network
    domestic: fixed-line services provided by multiple telecommunications operators; fixed-line teledensity stands at about 15 per 100 persons; mobile-cellular use has surged and subscribership has reached 100 per 100 persons
    international: country code - 593; landing points for the PAN-AM and South America-1 submarine cables that provide links to the west coast of South America, Panama, Colombia, Venezuela, and extending onward to Aruba and the US Virgin Islands in the Caribbean;

satellite earth station - 1 Intelsat (Atlantic Ocean) (2011)

**Broadcast media:**
Ecuador has multiple TV networks and many local channels, as well as more than 300 radio stations; many TV and radio stations are privately owned; the government owns or controls 5 national TV stations and multiple radio stations; broadcast media required by law to give the government free air time to broadcast programs produced by the state (2007)

**Internet country code:**
.ec

**Internet hosts:**
170,538 (2012)
country comparison to the world: 76

**Internet users:**
3.352 million (2009)
country comparison to the world: 64

# Chapter 8: Transportation

**Airports:**

    432 (2013)

    country comparison to the world: 20

**Airports - with paved runways:**

    total: 104

    over 3,047 m: 4

    2,438 to 3,047 m: 5

    1,524 to 2,437 m: 18

    914 to 1,523 m: 26

    under 914 m: 51 (2013)

**Airports - with unpaved runways:**

    total: 328

    914 to 1,523 m: 37

    under 914 m: 291 (2013)

**Heliports:**

    2 (2013)

**Pipelines:**

    extra heavy crude 527 km; gas 71 km; oil 2,131 km; refined products 1,526 km (2013)

**Railways:**
total: 965 km
country comparison to the world: 90
narrow gague: 965 km 1.067-m gauge (2008)

**Roadways:**
total: 43,670 km
country comparison to the world: 84

**Waterways:**
1,500 km (most inaccessible) (2012)
country comparison to the world: 53

**Merchant marine:**
total: 44
country comparison to the world: 72
by type: cargo 1, chemical tanker 4, liquefied gas 1, passenger 9, petroleum tanker 28, refrigerated cargo 1
registered in other countries: 4 (Panama 3, Peru 1) (2010)

**Ports and terminals:**
Major seaports: Esmeraldas, Manta, Puerto Bolivar
River ports: Guayaquil (Guayas)
Container ports (TEUs): Guayaquil (2,405,762)

# Chapter 9: Military

**Military branches:**
Ecuadorian Armed Forces: Ecuadorian Land Force (Fuerza Terrestre Ecuatoriana, FTE), Ecuadorian Navy (Fuerza Naval del Ecuador (FNE), includes Naval Infantry, Naval Aviation, Coast Guard), Ecuadorian Air Force (Fuerza Aerea Ecuatoriana, FAE) (2012)

**Military service age and obligation:**
18 years of age for selective conscript military service; conscription has been suspended; 18 years of age for voluntary military service; Air Force 18-22 years of age, Ecadorian birth requirement; 1-year service obligation (2012)

**Manpower available for military service:**
males age 16-49: 3,728,906
females age 16-49: 3,844,918 (2010 est.)

**Manpower fit for military service:**
males age 16-49: 2,834,213
females age 16-49: 3,269,535 (2010 est.)

**Manpower reaching militarily significant age annually:**
male: 152,593
female: 147,143 (2010 est.)

**Military expenditures:**
2.83% of GDP (2012)
country comparison to the world: 52

# Chapter 10: Transnational Issues

**Disputes - international:**
> Organized illegal narcotics operations in Colombia penetrate across Ecuador's shared border, which thousands of Colombians also cross to escape the violence in their home country

**Refugees and internally displaced persons:**
> Refugees (country of origin): 122,964 (Colombia) (2012)

**Illicit drugs:**
> significant transit country for cocaine originating in Colombia and Peru, with much of the US-bound cocaine passing through Ecuadorian Pacific waters; importer of precursor chemicals used in production of illicit narcotics; attractive location for cash-placement by drug traffickers laundering money because of dollarization and weak anti-money-laundering regime; increased activity on the northern frontier by trafficking groups and Colombian insurgents (2008)

# Map of Ecuador

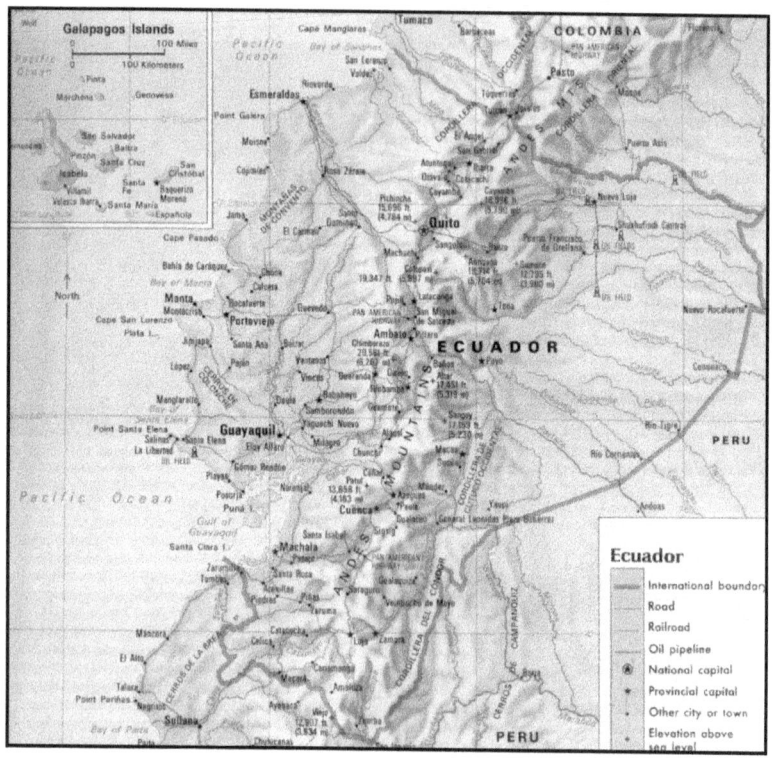

# Other Key Facts™ Titles

Key Facts on Syria

Key Facts on China

Key Facts on Qatar

Key Facts on India

Key Facts on Germany

Key Facts on Argentina

Key Facts on Russia

Key Facts on North Korea

Key Facts on Brazil

Key Facts on Italy

Key Facts on the United Arab Emirates

Key Facts on the European Union

Key Facts on Pakistan

Key Facts on Saudi Arabia

Key Facts on Cyprus

Key Facts on Iran

Key Facts on Afghanistan

Key Facts on Iraq

Key Facts on Indonesia

Key Facts on South Korea

Key Facts on France

Key Facts on the United Kingdom

Key Facts on Egypt

Key Facts on Israel

All Key Facts™ Titles are Available at

www.Amazon.com

THE INTERNATIONALIST®
2013
WWW.INTERNATIONALIST.COM